What Happened to the Gifts?

Written by: Lois Chipman-Sullivan

Illustrated by: Rosemarie Gillen

Copyright © 2010 by Lois Chipman-Sullivan

What Happened to the Gifts?
by Lois Chipman-Sullivan

Printed in the United States of America

ISBN 9781609578305

All rights reserved solely by the author. The author guarantees all contents are original and do not infringe upon the legal rights of any other person or work. No part of this book may be reproduced in any form without the permission of the author. The views expressed in this book are not necessarily those of the publisher.

www.xulonpress.com

What Happened to the Gifts?
By Lois Chipman-Sullivan

This book has been a project of love. Along the journey, I had two very important and special partners. First is my husband, John L. Sullivan, (Sully), who has been my never-wavering supporter and confidant. He shares my passion for family, faith and adventure. Together we have enjoyed life and look forward to many more adventures together and with our family. Family is Forever.

Second is Father Robert Hoeffner, our Pastor from St. Joseph's Catholic Church in Palm Bay, Florida. Father Bob has provided John and me with many wonderfully spiritual moments through his true gift of sharing the Word of Jesus Christ. He brings joy and laughter to the Scriptures, along with peace and prodding. We shared this book with Father Bob before "going to press" to gain his perspective. He will always remain in our prayers and hearts.

The subject of this book came to me one day as we were putting away our Christmas decorations. I started wondering about the Magi Story. And thought, What Happened to the Gifts? So this book began. It was not meant to be a theological research project but an inner discovery of what gift-giving can mean, even at the time that Jesus was born. Along this journey, I was truly blessed to find Rosemarie Gillen to bring my story to life with her warm and gentle illustrations. We have shared in the fulfillment of my dream and I thank her with all of my heart.

I wanted to share this special time and message with my grandchildren as they began their journey through life. So, to JM, Sean, David, Katarina, Lauren, Mara, Leah, Saylor and all my grandchildren yet to come, I dedicate this book. A simple story about the most important event in history and how we can still participate.
~Enjoy.

"Look who is here under the Star! I see the new Savior, Jesus," said the Angel Krystal.

"Yes, look how happy they are. Joseph and Mary are so pleased to be the parents of Jesus. They know this is such a wonderful night. It is the beginning of a whole new world," said the Angel Chippitt.

"Oh, yes, Jesus can bring Peace and Love to everyone," said the Angel Junie.

"Look at how Mary and Joseph are taking care of Jesus. They are really a Holy Family. I know they are going to have many blessings raising such a wonderful Son as Jesus. He will certainly bring Peace and Love to the world," said the Angel Krystal.

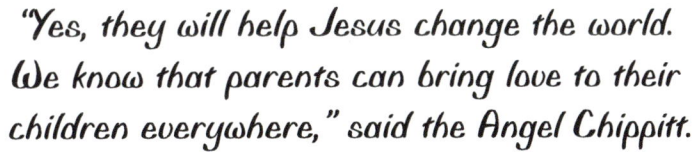

"Yes, they will help Jesus change the world. We know that parents can bring love to their children everywhere," said the Angel Chippitt.

"But who else knows that they are here? Oh look! Here comes some special visitors!" said the Angel Junie.

"Wow, it's three Kings and they have beautiful coats and crowns! I'm sure they have come from far away places to visit Jesus. They must have heard about the Savior, Jesus, and want to welcome him, too," said the Angel Chippitt.

"Look, they are bringing Jesus some special gifts. What do you think they could be? Let's look a little closer," said the Angel Krystal.

"I think that I can see why the gifts are really special. I see some gold! It can make them rich! They can get many things for Jesus to play with and make him happy. That is really a special gift!"
said the Angel Krystal.

"Oh, look, I also see some frankincense. I know what that is. It comes from a special tree and helps make people who are sick feel better. What a wonderful gift to receive. It is good to help other people,"
said the Angel Chippitt.

"Now I can see the third gift and it looks like myrrh," said the Angel Junie.

"Oh, I know about myrrh. All the angels talk about myrrh. It is a holy oil that helps to get people ready when they are coming home to Jesus in Heaven," said the Angel Krystal.

"I can see that the Three Kings are leaving to go home. It looks like the Holy Family is getting ready to leave, too," said the Angel Krystal.

"Yes, they are getting all their belongings together. What are they going to do with their wonderful gifts?" said the Angel Chippitt.

"Do you think they can use the gifts to bring Peace and Love to the World like Jesus will teach us about?" said the Angel Junie.

"Oh, I can see that they are going to leave the gifts in the manger. They think it would be better to not take the gifts from the Three Kings. The gifts might change the Family too much. Or, maybe, they might look so rich that their friends will not like them anymore. They think it would be better to just leave without the gifts," said the Angel Krystal.

"I don't think they are going to leave the gifts there. Look, Mary is packing them up. I think they are going to take the gifts with them to help the Family. If they take them with them, they can use the gifts to help Jesus and give him many things to make him happy. I'm sure that is what they are going to do!" said the Angel Chippitt.

"Oh wait, I can see what they are going to do! Joseph is giving some of the gifts to the shepherds who are helping them to go back to their home. They are sharing the gifts," said the Angel Junie.

"Well, I think that they should leave the gifts. It would be best for everyone. They will be happier without all of those gifts. When we get special gifts, we don't have to keep them, even if they are from Kings,"
said the Angel Krystal.

"Oh, I'm not so sure about that. If the Family keeps the gifts from the Kings they can do more things for Jesus so he is happy and safe,"
said the Angel Chippitt.

"Well, I'm not sure what is the best thing to do with the gifts. I saw Joseph giving some of the gifts to the shepherds. I just don't know what they should do. How can these gifts help to bring Peace and Love to the World? Who can tell us what they should do?" said the Angel Junie.

"My friends, I can see that you are having trouble deciding what Mary and Joseph should do with their gifts. Remember that the most special gifts we receive are the teachings of Jesus. His teachings are God's special gifts to everyone everywhere. He teaches us to be kind, caring, and loving to all people. When we love each other and take care of each other, we can help to make all people happy and bring Peace and Love to the World," said the Angel Gabriel.

"What would happen if God's special gifts were left at the manger? They would be forgotten and not used by anyone. If the Holy Family uses all their gifts for themselves, it could make their lives better but no one else's. Now, if the Family shares their gifts from God and their gifts from the Kings with their friends and neighbors, they can help others and spread the Words of Jesus. So, my Angels, what do you think the Family should do to help Jesus spread Peace and Love to the World?" said the Angel Gabriel.

"Share all the gifts! Share the Kings's gifts!
Share God's special gifts!" shouted all the Angels.

"My yes, you are all right! Sharing God's special gifts
that he brings to each of us will spread the teachings of
Jesus. It will help to bring Peace and Love to everyone in the World. Now
it is time for you all to greet Jesus and begin helping others learn
about Jesus and how to share his gifts," said the Angel Gabriel.

"What gifts has Jesus given to you?
How will you share them?
How can you help others?"

LaVergne, TN USA
03 October 2010
199230LV00003B